# Ships of the Isle of Man Steam Packet Company

*by*
Steven Dearden and Ken Hassell

By the turn of the century the Victoria Pier displayed the familiar bustle that is to be seen on dozens of Edwardian postcards. There was no shelter available at this stage, nor any control of passengers. It wasn't necessary to book on a crossing beforehand – you just walked on board and about an hour after sailing the purser and his assistants came round to collect the fares.

*Mona's Isle* was the first vessel owned by the Isle of Man Steam Packet Company. Under the command of William Gill she established the superiority of the Manx company over the rival St George Steam Packet Company.

*Queen of the Isle* was the third vessel in the company's fleet and said to be the fastest on the Irish Sea in her day.




First published in the United Kingdom, 1999,
by Stenlake Publishing, Ochiltree Sawmill, The Lade,
Ochiltree, Ayrshire, KA18 2NX
Telephone / Fax: 01290 423114

ISBN 1 84033 078 3



**Dates in brackets denote a vessel's length of service with the company.**

## FURTHER READING

The books listed below were used by the authors during their research. None of them are available from Stenlake Publishing. Those interested in finding out more are advised to contact their local bookshop or reference library.

Blackburn, C. J., *How the Manx Fleet Helped in the Great War*, 1923 (reprinted 1993).
*Centenary of the Isle of Man Steam Packet Company*, 1930.
Chappell, Connery, *Island Lifeline*, 1980.
Goodwyn, A. M., *Eight Decades of Heysham-Douglas*, 1985.
Hallam, W. B., *Fifteen Decades of Service to Man*, (*Sea Breezes*, September to November 1980, vol. 54, nos. 417-419).
Henry, Fred, *Ships of the Isle of Man Steam Packet Company*, 5 editions, 1962-1987.
Moore, A. W., *Historical Account of the Isle of Man Steam Packet Company*, 1904.
Shepherd, John, *The Life and Times of the Steam Packet*, 1994.
*Manxlink* – magazine for enthusiasts of IOM Steam Packet ships.

# INTRODUCTION

A degree of regularity first came to communications with the Isle of Man in 1767 when the British government established a regular weekly packet boat for the conveyance of passengers and mail between Douglas and Whitehaven. This move was not unconnected with the purchase of the Island from the Duke of Atholl two years earlier.

The regularity of sailings still depended on the weather and contact with the mainland could be very uncertain in winter. In 1828 the mail service was transferred to Liverpool and the St George Steam Packet Company, whose winter service, operated by its oldest and slowest steamers without even basic shelter for passengers, increased discontent to the point where a meeting was held in Douglas on 17 December 1829 to appoint a committee to ascertain the probable cost of a steam packet run by and for Island interests.

The Mona's Isle Company was set up to this end, its name changing in January 1832 to The Isle of Man United Steam Packet Company (the 'United' was dropped in July of the same year). 'Limited' was added in 1885 and the company provided a vital 'Island lifeline' until its amalgamation with Sealink in 1985 and take-over by Sea Containers Ltd. in 1996. This sadly marked its end as a wholly Manx-owned concern, although it had outlived all its competitors to become the oldest shipping line in the British coastal fleets.

The company's first steamer, the *Mona's Isle*, was launched on 30 June 1830, inaugurating the Douglas to Liverpool service on 16 August, when she carried 15 saloon and 17 steerage passengers. Although small, she was fast for her day, averaging eight hours for the passage. Competition and a fierce price war with the St George's Company came to an end with the wreck of the *St George* on Conister Rock on 20 November 1830. The mail contract was awarded to the Steam Packet the following year and a period of gradual expansion, free from serious competition for fifty years, commenced. Initially an average of 10,000 passengers were carried annually, rising to 100,000 by 1875 after the opening of the Victoria Pier ended the difficulties in landing and embarking large numbers of passengers at Douglas. Numbers continued to grow with the size and number of steamers. They peaked in 1913 when 1,152,048 passengers were carried to a wide range of destinations by 14 steamers covering 2,431 trips and 177,958 miles.

This book does not attempt to provide a comprehensive history of the company – details of such histories can be found in the Further Reading. Instead we have presented a photographic record of the ships that sailed in the heyday of the service, when the boom in the tourist industry was interrupted only by the First World War, and during which the Steam Packet's ships made valuable contributions to the war effort. All the ships that sailed between 1900 and 1940 are included here, during a period that began with paddle steamers reigning supreme and ended just before the last phase of classic steamers were constructed.

This was perhaps the final period when the full magic of a voyage to the Isle of Man could be experienced. It really was as near to 'going abroad' as the majority of holidaymakers could dream of; from the messages on the backs of their postcards it appears that it was to be approached with much trepidation and a clear expectation that seasickness was inevitable.

Arnold Bennett described the emotions to be experienced at Liverpool in his novel *Anna of the Five Towns*:

> The great, wavy river, churned by thousands of keels, the monstrous steamer – the *Mona's Isle* – whose side rose like a solid wall out of the water, the vistas of its decks, its vast saloons, storey upon storey, solid and palatial (could all this float?), its high bridge, its hawsers as thick as trees, the multitudes of passengers, the whistles, hoots, cries, the far-stretching panorama of wharves and docks, the squat ferry-craft carrying horses and carts, and no one looking twice at the feat – it was all too much, too astonishing, too lovely.

The steamers were described as floating palaces, with everything possible done to make the short trip pleasant. The majority of passengers preferred the open deck where small card parties took place and others read or chatted while strains of music floated gently on the air from a band. A more agreeable way of crossing the Irish Sea could not be imagined. We hope that some of this magic can be recaptured in the photographs that follow.

The *Ellan Vannin* began her life as the iron paddle steamer *Mona's Isle II* in 1860, being converted to a twin screw steamer in 1882 and renamed the following year. She was particularly connected with the Ramsey route and is seen here to the left assisting the SS *Antrim* in successfully pulling the SS *Donegal* off the shore near the gravel jetty at the Point of Ayre. The *Donegal* had run aground in thick fog on the night of 2 October 1908 on passage from Heysham to Belfast. The *Ellan Vannin*, captained by James Teare, was noted as the most useful and probably one of the most profitable vessels ever owned by the company, although her life ended tragically when on 3 December 1909 she sank with all hands on the Mersey Bar. 21 crew and 15 passengers were lost.

The *Tynwald* of 1866 was a fast vessel that uniquely had both funnels abaft the paddle boxes. The early years of the company were not without controversy, the treatment of passengers prior to the provision of the deep-water pier being particularly open to criticism. On one occasion in 1869 the *Tynwald* arrived at low water at 6.15 p.m. with 700 passengers. Unable to come alongside the pier, it was almost 8 o'clock before the last passengers were landed. It was reported that the small boats taking the passengers off were dangerously overcrowded, and that customers also had to put up with the 'vicious, blasphemous and horrible language of the ruffianly fellows in charge of the boats'. In January 1887 the *Tynwald* collided in the Mersey with the Birkenhead ferry *Lancashire* and, although repaired and able to convey the new Douglas lifeboat *Thomas Rose* to the Island, she was soon auctioned for scrap, made redundant by the acquisition of the *Queen Victoria* and *Prince of Wales*.

Built in 1871 by R. Duncan & Co. of Glasgow, the *King Orry*'s entry into service coincided with the completion of the Victoria Pier, a facility that led to a great increase in traffic and also eventually attracted competition from rival companies. This postcard shows her after 1888 when her length was increased from 260 to 290 feet and tonnage from 806 to 1,104 tons. After 41 years service, a record at the time, she was broken up at Lanerchymer in 1912. The *King Orry* was taken there by Captain Quine and the vessel was opened to the public before scrapping, raising money for the local hospital.

The *Ben-my-Chree* was the first vessel in the fleet of over 1,000 tons and, constructed at Barrow, only the second vessel to have been built away from the Clyde (the first having been the original *King Orry*). At 14 knots she was a slow vessel, never reaching her contract speed. During a major overhaul in 1884 she was reboilered, lengthened and two additional funnels were fitted – one fore and one aft of the paddle boxes. Unmistakable in appearance, this photograph shows her by the Imperial Hotel, head office of the Steam Packet until 1969. The extra funnels added to her popularity but unfortunately without particularly increasing her speed. In August 1901 she collided with the Powell steamer *West Coast* in the Crosby Channel and was broken up at Morecambe in August 1906.

An iron paddle steamer, the *Snaefell* gave 38 years of steady service to the company, the only incident she was involved in being a collision with the Norwegian vessel *Keleb* on her way to Ardrossan in August 1892. She was launched on 27 April 1876 to replace the first *Snaefell*, which had been sold the previous year. She served two charters, the first in 1876 to the Zeeland Steamship Company, buyers of the *Snaefell I*, the second in 1890 to the Great Western Railway Company. The Royal Mersey Yacht Club also chartered her as their headquarters ship for several regattas. The *Snaefell* was broken up in Holland in 1904.

The *Fenella*, acquired in 1881 from the Barrow Ship Building Co., was the last iron vessel and the first twin screw steamer in the fleet. She was intended for general cargo work in the summer and passenger service in the winter, which meant she was worked particularly hard. Notorious for rolling in heavy weather, a regular winter passenger recalled his heart sinking when tickets were collected as passengers boarded – a sure sign of rough weather to come. The sound of a crate of broken crockery careering across the saloon accompanied the unlucky passengers throughout the passage. Crossing from Douglas to Liverpool in February 1895 she arrived very late in a blizzard with her hull, masts and funnel completely ice-covered. At the inquiry following the loss of the *Ellan Vannin* (which claimed 36 lives), it was noted that the only previous occasion on which the company had suffered loss of life was on 1 January 1899 when three passengers who refused to go below were washed off the *Fenella*. After 48 years service *Fenella* was disposed of in 1929 at the same time as the *Mona's Queen II*, the last of the paddle steamers.

The *Mona's Isle III* was the first steel ship in the fleet and the first of five similar paddle steamers. She was not only much larger, but also three-quarters of an hour faster than her predecessors. In 1884 Prime Minister William Gladstone, a visitor to the Island, was so impressed with her that he requested permission to inspect her. Her service was not without incident; she was stranded north of Ramsey in April 1883, at Scarlet Point in September 1892, and she sustained serious damage to her paddle wheels in heavy seas en route to Liverpool in May 1885. She was chartered for a special cruise from Southampton to see the Review of the Fleet at Spithead for the Coronation of King Edward VII on 28 June 1902. 1911 saw her conveying a large quantity of bullion to Liverpool under the armed escort of the cruiser HMS *Warrior*. Requisitioned by the Admiralty in 1915 and converted to a net layer, the *Mona's Isle* was scrapped in 1919.

The *Mona's Queen*, built in response to competition from the Isle of Man, Liverpool and Manchester Steamship Company, became the last surviving paddle steamer in the Steam Packet's fleet. She served on the Fleetwood station from 1885 to 1886 and 1889 to 1904, covering the Liverpool route during a severe period of competition during 1887 and 1888. By 1925 she was employed at weekends only, filling in with 'Round the Island' excursions. Her last passenger trip was from Fleetwood to Douglas on 31 August 1929. This T. H. Midwood photograph shows her arriving at Ramsey laden with soldiers for one of the pre-war Territorial Army camps at Milntown.

This second picture shows the *Mona's Queen* at Weymouth in her wartime colours on her way back home. The card is dated 3 February 1919, and the writer says 'arrived at this place safe and sound and we are leaving for Liverpool today'. The highlight of her wartime service came when she sank a U-boat in February 1917. Despite having a torpedo fired at his ship, Capt. William Cain succeeded in smashing open the submarine's hull with the paddle wheel.

The *Queen Victoria* was built with the *Prince of Wales* for the Isle of Man, Liverpool and Manchester Steamship Company (popularly known as the Manx Line). Both vessels were three knots faster than any of the Steam Packet's and when racing took place between the rival companies they repeatedly proved half an hour faster. The vessels were built in 1887 and the intention was always to force the Steam Packet to buy the new company out, the Fairfield Company having set up the Manx Line specifically to prove the superiority of their compound diagonal type of engine for paddle steamers. Crowds flocked to the new ships and their cut-price fares, one day in May 1888 seeing 1,000 passengers left behind and many injured in trying to board ship. With return fares at 5/- first class and 2/6 second class saloon, both companies lost money, and at the end of the season the Steam Packet bought the two Manx Line ships, also ordering a new vessel, the *Tynwald III*, from the same builders.

The second of the Manx Line ships, the *Prince of Wales* made the journey from the Mersey to Douglas Head in 2 hours 59 minutes on one occasion. Captain Owen Lewis had commanded the *Queen Victoria* for Manx Line and he followed the ships to the Steam Packet, where he was appointed to the *Prince of Wales*. As the fastest ship in the fleet, *Prince of Wales* sailed daily from Liverpool at 11.30 a.m. and returned from Douglas at 4 p.m., being at anchor by 7.40 p.m. On at least one occasion three passages totalling 225 miles were made in under 12 hours. The *Prince of Wales* was sold to the Admiralty as a net layer in 1915, being renamed the *Prince Edward*. Along with the *Queen Victoria* she did not return to the Steam Packet, and both vessels were broken up in 1920.

The *Tynwald III* was ordered from the Fairfield Company as a direct result of the success of the *Queen Victoria* and the *Prince of Wales*, although as a twin screw steamer she was considerably smaller than the paddle steamers. She was also the first ship to be fitted with electric light. The *Tynwald* was particularly associated with the Ardrossan service but in July 1912 inaugurated a service from Douglas to Ramsey and Whitehaven. In 1914 she carried the first German internees to the Island and in 1916 conveyed troops to Dublin to suppress the Easter Rebellion. On 9 April 1917 she rescued 60 passengers from the liner *New York* when it was mined near the Mersey Bar. The *Tynwald* continued to give valuable service until, after some unsuccessful Blackpool-based excursions in 1930, she was laid up at Barrow and sold. She was bought by R. A. Colby Cubbin of Douglas, who intended to convert her to a private yacht, but she was requisitioned in 1939 and after lying in Wallasey Dock for many years was finally scrapped in 1951.

Named to commemorate the diamond jubilee of Queen Victoria, the *Empress Queen* was the largest, fastest and most powerful coasting paddle steamer ever built, with her engines and paddle wheels the heaviest ever fitted. Her crew numbered 110, including 50 stewards, and she had a passenger-carrying capacity of 2,000. A particular feature, visible in this photograph of her leaving Douglas, was the promenade deck over the upper deck, roofed over to allow travellers to remain in the open even in wet weather. Her first year in service, 1897, saw her break the Liverpool to Douglas record, and in 1903 she became the first Steam Packet ship to be fitted with Marconi wireless. The *Empress Queen* was wrecked on the coast of the Isle of Wight on 1 February 1916 whilst acting as a troop transporter.

The *Douglas* was purchased second-hand to replace the *Peveril* which had sunk in 1899. The purchase was an innovation for the company, who with the exception of the almost new and particularly suitable *Prince of Wales* and *Queen Victoria* had always had new vessels built. Formerly the *Dora*, built in 1889 for the London and South Western Railway Company's Channel Islands service, she entered Steam Packet service in 1901. During the 1914-1918 war she maintained the Island lifeline along with the *Fenella* and the *Tynwald*. The *Douglas* sank on 16 August 1923 after a collision with the *Artemisia* off Herculaneum Dock, Liverpool. Loss of life was only prevented by the *Artemisia* keeping her engines running while the *Douglas*'s 15 passengers and crew were saved by the Mersey tug *Fighting Cock*. If the engines had been reversed or turned off the *Douglas* would have filled with water; it was only by the *Artemisia* covering the gaping hole that time was gained to get everyone off. A subsequent enquiry found defective navigation by the *Douglas* to be to blame for the sinking.

In 1899 Mr S. W. Higginbottom, a Liverpool MP and colliery owner, formed a rival company, Liverpool and Douglas Steamers Ltd. He put two Irish ships on the Liverpool to Douglas station and acquired several other cross channel steamers. Price cutting broke out again with the new company offering saloon return tickets at 4/- and steerage 3/- with a free bottle of beer included. Large sums of money were wagered and racing resumed between rival ships. Higginbottom's only successful purchase, however, was the *Calais-Douvres*, built by the Fairfield Shipping Company in 1889. On his death in December 1902 she was bought by the Steam Packet and renamed the *Mona III*. The last paddle steamer to be acquired, the *Mona* was sold for scrap after only six years and broken up at Briton Ferry in 1909.

The success of the *Viking* (featured on the front cover), put into service in 1905, led to the order of a larger turbine steamer from the Vickers, Sons and Maxim Ltd. Barrow yard. These two pictures were taken at the launch of the *Ben-my-Chree* on 23 March 1908. The ceremony was performed by Mrs I. T. Cowell. Ordered for the Liverpool to Douglas service, the *Ben-my-Chree* was the fastest and most powerful vessel ever built for the company and her crew of 116 was probably the largest ever employed on such a coastal vessel.

The vertical picture shows final preparations being made for the *Ben-my-Chree*'s trial runs in July 1908, when she attained a speed of 26.64 knots and the distinction of being the fastest steamer in British home waters. After the trials she was docked at Birkenhead and made her inaugural passage to Douglas on 15 July. The 1908 season was the busiest the company had ever enjoyed, with the total number of passengers carried by the fleet exceeding 1,000,000, and the *Ben-my-Chree* carrying her full complement of 2,550 passengers on several voyages. She still holds the Liverpool to Douglas record for a conventional vessel – 2 hours 57 minutes – and in 1911 was chosen for the proposed race around the Island against pioneer aviator Claude Graham-White. The weather was unkind to Graham-White, but the *Ben-my-Chree* completed her journey in a record 2 hours 56 minutes. Commissioned in 1915 as a seaplane carrier, she made history when a plane launched from her deck became the first to torpedo and sink a ship. Her loss to Turkish gunfire off Castellorizo on 11 January 1917 caused more grief to the Manx people than any other. A verse from a song of the time, *The Steamers Three*, ran:

My heart is sad for the Ben-my-Chree
She was sunk by the foe in the open sea
God bless the souls of her gallant crew
They were good Manx sailors, faithful and true.

The *Snaefell III* was launched from Cammell Lairds, Birkenhead on 12 February 1910 (see overleaf). Her trial trip followed on 25 July when she reached Douglas Bay in under three hours, discharging several rockets before putting about and returning to the Bar lightship in heavy seas, where she was 'manoeuvred in every direction with ease'. Her first service trip, under Captain Bridson, followed on 28 July when many people crossed over from the Island on the *Prince of Wales* that morning specifically to be on the maiden voyage. This T. H. Midwood photograph shows her at Ramsey, watched by the large crowd of locals and visitors that a departure usually attracted.

The *Snaefell III* was intended to maintain the winter service, working from Ramsey as well as Douglas on the secondary routes during the summer. Sadly, she was to see only four years service, as having been requisitioned as an armed boarding vessel she was torpedoed off Alexandria on her way to Malta on 5 June 1918.

Built by J. Fullerton of Paisley in 1892, the *Tyrconnel* was first registered in Glasgow, then Londonderry, before being bought by the Manx Steam Trading Company of Castletown in 1902. When purchased by the Steam Packet in 1911 she became the first purely cargo vessel in the fleet. As seen in this B. & A. Fielden postcard, she retained her non-standard yellow, black topped funnel right through her service. The 1912 Steam Packet guide advertised her as sailing once weekly from Salthouse Dock, Liverpool, conveying cargo to Castletown, Port St Mary and Peel. She was disposed of to S. W. Coe in 1932 and broken up in 1934.

The *Ramsey* was built in 1895 for the Lancashire and Yorkshire Railway Co., who operated her on the Fleetwood to Belfast service as the *Duke of Lancaster*, along with the *Duke of York* (later the *Peel Castle*). She was bought by the Steam Packet in July 1912 from the Turkish Patriotic Committee who had been unable to take delivery of her due to the outbreak of war between Turkey and Italy. This Midwood photograph shows her in Ramsey harbour on what was to prove an extremely short stay with the company. Requisitioned by the Admiralty in September 1914, she served in the North Sea as HMS *Ramsey*, and was sunk with the loss of 52 lives on 7 August 1915. A broadside from the armed raider *Meteor* killed her commander and officers; a torpedo then hit the crew quarters, sinking the vessel in less than four minutes. The survivors escaped internment when the *Meteor* was abandoned and deliberately blown up to avoid capture two days later.

Built in 1894 as the *Duke of York*, the *Peel Castle* was the second vessel obtained from the Turkish Patriotic Committee in 1912. Also requisitioned by the Admiralty, she survived mines, submarine attacks and a serious fire in February 1918 to return to give long and valuable service to the Island. For many years she maintained the direct Friday 2 p.m. sailing from Liverpool to Ramsey, as well as being used for cargo duties and excursion trips. During the Territorials' camping season she was occasionally used as a hospital training ship and in this V. L. Swales postcard she is acting as tender to the White Star liner *Albertic* on the occasion of the 1927 'Manx Homecoming'. These reunions of ex-patriot Manx from North America and beyond proved extremely popular, and three years later *Peel Castle* repeated the service for the *Doric*. She was broken up on the Clyde in February 1939.

The last ship built for the company before World War I, the *King Orry* was constructed by Cammell Laird at Birkenhead at a cost of £96,000 with accommodation for 1,600 passengers and 59 crew. Launched on 11 March 1913, her trials took place on 27 June when a speed of 20.94 knots was achieved. On her way back she called into Douglas Bay to a rousing welcome from the *Ramsey*, *Viking* and *Ben-my-Chree*. She is seen here leaving Birkenhead to enter service on 8 July 1913.

In common with so many Steam Packet vessels, *King Orry* was quickly requisitioned, and left Birkenhead on 27 November 1914 for Scapa Flow. As the armed boarding steamer *Viking Orry* she survived many dangers, including a stranding on Islay and severe gale damage in the Pentland Firth to become the only one of the converted passenger ferries on these duties to emerge unscathed. This was all the more lucky as each time she left port her Plimsoll mark was submerged, on account of the 220 tons of extra coal which had to be stored. She is seen here on her later troop-carrying duties between Southampton and the French ports. The *King Orry*'s greatest moment came on 21 November 1918 when she steamed into the Firth of Forth between the surrendered battleships of the German High Seas Fleet.

After early incidents such as hitting the Victoria Pier and striking the coaster *St Margaret* at Dublin in July 1914, the rest of *King Orry*'s peacetime career passed without major incident, except for the occasion shown on this photograph taken by Tierney's of Liverpool. While entering the Mersey in dense fog the *King Orry* went aground at New Brighton on 19 August 1921. Fortunately she come off undamaged after a few hours, the passengers having been disembarked via a series of ladders supplied by locals, a process that generated great interest amongst onlooking holidaymakers. The *King Orry* finally met her end when she was dive-bombed on her second trip to Dunkirk on 29 May 1940.

The *Mona* also suffered a grounding in thick fog during her time with the Steam Packet; this occurred on Conister Rock on 2 July 1930. Passengers were disembarked into small boats and she was pulled off during the night, only narrowly missing the Battery Pier. Built in 1907 as the *Hazel* for the Ardrossan-Portrush route of the Laird Line, the *Mona* was purchased in 1919 to replace vessels lost in the war. Largely used on cargo runs and winter service, her career was eventful, and included ramming the Crosby lightship in the Mersey on one occasion. During blizzards in February 1929 she was diverted to Peel, but was unable to land her passengers. They stayed on board all night only to find themselves stranded on landing because the roads and railway line were blocked.

During the war, eleven of the Steam Packet steamers were chartered or purchased by the Admiralty, and of these four were lost and three retained by the government. Even with the purchase of the *Mona*, this only gave the company a capacity of 9,500 passengers, as against the pre-war figure of about 20,000. During the 1919 season the *La Marguerite* was chartered from the Liverpool and North Wales Steamship Company to cope with the resurgent tourist traffic. The vessel, no stranger to the Island, enjoyed a successful season and is seen here with her funnels painted Steam Packet red with black tops rather than their usual yellow.

The *Manxman*, photographed in her original Midland Railway colours. *Manxman* was built for the Midland Railway's Heysham to Douglas service in 1904, and her sister ships the *Donegal*, *Antrim* and *Londonderry* were all regular visitors to the Island. She was a very reliable vessel, designed by Sir John H. Biles, who was responsible for transatlantic liners such as the *City of New York*, *Armenia* and *City of Paris*, built for the Inman Line.

The *Manxman*'s cabin staff of 1910, photographed during the vessel's service with the Midland Railway. Prices of goods available on the steamers have often come in for criticism, but those of the 1910 season belong to another world. A four course dinner cost 2/6d, breakfast or a plate of meat 1/-, sandwiches 2d or 4d, a cup of tea 3d and a cake 2d. Whisky, rum or gin was 3½d – almost the same price as mineral waters – whilst the most expensive item was a quart of champagne for 9/- or 10/6d.

The *Manxman* was bought by the Steam Packet in 1920. She was in poor condition following war service, and was refurbished and converted to oil fuel in 1921. This enabled her to maintain service during the General Strike of 1926 when it was almost impossible for coal-fired ships to operate. This animated 1937 photograph shows her at Prince's Landing Stage, Liverpool, with the Steam Packet booking office on the far right. During the Second World War *Manxman* served as the RDF training ship HMS *Caduceus* and was sent to Douglas, where after two collisions with the Victoria Pier, the navy seemingly allowed Steam Packet officers temporary commissions to navigate her and other ships safely into Douglas harbour.

The *Onward* was built in 1905 for the South Eastern and Chatham Railway's cross-channel services, and took her name from the railway company's motto. She was bought by the Steam Packet in May 1920, having been scuttled at Folkestone after a fire caused by an enemy saboteur. The Steam Packet found that the only ships available after the war were close to being total losses. Leaving Union Dock, Limehouse, *Onward*(later renamed *Mona's Isle*) made history as the first vessel to fly the Manx flag down the Thames.

Renamed during 1920, her first year of service, the *Mona's Isle* served mostly on the Douglas to Dublin or Belfast services. She served right through to 1939 when, commandeered again, she became the first ship to make a round trip to Dunkirk, sustaining serious damage in doing so. She was reconditioned in 1945 but was increasingly only used as a reserve ship, being broken up in 1948.

Another 1920 purchase was the *Viper*, built in 1905 and operated between Belfast and Ardrossan by G. & J. Burns. On her return from duties as a troop transporter, her old route having been abandoned, she came on the market and entered Steam Packet service in July 1920. As the *Snaefell* she served on many routes, replacing the *Victoria* on the Douglas to Heysham service in 1933. She maintained the difficult Douglas to Fleetwood wartime service with the *Rushen Castle* and was finally withdrawn in 1945.

Built as the *Ardnagrena* in 1908, *Cushag* was first owned by James Waterson of County Antrim who sold her to Humber Steam Coasters in 1914. The Steam Packet bought her from a London broker in May 1920 and she became the first 'machinery aft' vessel in the fleet. Seen here at Peel in 1937, the *Cushag* was small enough to enter the harbour there and at Castletown, Port St Mary and Laxey. Wallace Squires of Lime Street, Port St Mary commanded her for many years. He was noted for rarely refusing anyone a trip on the local coastal sailings and the bridge was often crowded with holidaymakers or local lads, complete with bicycles for the return journey. The *Cushag* was sold in 1943 to Bremner & Co. of Kirkwall and was broken up in 1957.

Of the thirteen vessels in the fleet in 1920, only five had been built for the company and the average age was 22 years. The loss of the *Douglas* in 1923 caused severe problems, and the Steam Packet quickly bought the 1910 SS *Caesarea*. She was in need of extensive repairs herself, having been stranded on the Jersey coast that July. The repairs and conversion to oil fuel took place at Barrow, and she quickly proved her worth during the General Strike by maintaining the service with the only other oil burning ship, the *Manxman*. Seen here at Fleetwood in about 1935, the *Manx Maid* (as she was renamed) came through the war safely, despite special duties such as acting as the target ship for aircraft training for the destruction of the *Tirpitz*. She was withdrawn at the end of the 1950 season.

The *Manxman* developed a steering fault in July 1925 at the height of the holiday season, and this led to two short-term charters to enable the company to maintain a full range of services. The *Curraghmore* was chartered from the London, Midland and Scottish Railway for seven days and the Great Western Railway Company's *Menevia* from the last week in July to the end of August. These photographs were taken in Douglas during the vessels' short time with the Steam Packet Company.

The Steam Packet's post-war rebuilding programme started in 1927 with the *Ben-my-Chree*, the first of the famous steamers to be built between the wars. Her maiden voyage took place under Captain William Cain, Commodore of the Fleet, on 29 June 1927, her list of masters eventually including six commodores. Increased size and power added to the luxurious image of the new steamers, the saloon emerging from its traditional position below deck and the handsomely panelled first class lounge occupying the full width of the upper deck. The spacious decks could accommodate about 40 cars, an increasing advantage as the years passed. This D. Collister photograph shows the *Ben-my-Chree* leaving the Victoria Pier.

In 1932 the *Ben-my-Chree* was chartered by a North Lancashire Roman Catholic organisation to take passengers to a Eucharistic conference in Dublin. Her hull was supposedly painted white at Barrow specially for the occasion, and although the charter was eventually not taken up the effect proved so popular that she remained white until 1939. Indeed, the *Lady of Mann* and the *Mona's Queen* received similar treatment. A very busy war service included three trips to the Dunkirk evacuations and the landing of American troops on D-Day. The *Ben-my-Chree* continued in service until 1965.

The younger sister of *Mona's Isle IV*, the *Victoria* (built in 1907) was also purchased from the South Eastern and Chatham Railway, and was the third ship to be bought by the company in 1928. On 11 January 1919, while operating on the Dover to Calais service, she had had the distinction of conveying the Imperial delegation to the Versailles Peace Conference. She was purchased for the Heysham service, moving to the Belfast, Dublin and early season Liverpool sailings after a refit. Her original name was retained, and the *Victoria* acted as tender for the liner *Athenia* on the occasion of the 1937 Manx homecoming. Taken over by the Admiralty having been mined near the Mersey Bar in December 1940, she later landed troops on the famous Utah Beach during the 1944 Normandy landings.

In 1928 the company took over the Heysham and Douglas service, established in 1903 as the successor to the Barrow route and latterly conducted by the London, Midland and Scottish Railway. The Steam Packet acquired both vessels on the service, the *Duke of Cornwall* (which was renamed the *Rushen Castle*) and the *Antrim* of 1904, seen on the left at Heysham in her 'Midland' colours. Renamed *Ramsey Town*, she was not converted to oil fuel and, at nine seasons, her life with the Steam Packet was relatively short. She was broken up at Preston in 1936. Her winters were spent laid up at the Tongue in Douglas harbour, where she is seen in the second photograph next to one of the Douglas Head ferry boats.

The *Duke of Cornwall* was the second of the Heysham steamers. Dating from 1898 she was an older ship, but as the *Rushen Castle* she went on to serve the Steam Packet until 1947. This photograph shows her in Steam Packet colours under her original name.

The *Rushen Castle* covered the winter service to Liverpool between 1928 and 1936, and holds the record for the longest modern passage between Liverpool and Douglas – an incredible 71 hours in January 1940. She maintained the Fleetwood service throughout the war and in April 1946 became the first Isle of Man steamer to leave the Mersey since December 1940. In this B. & A. Fielden postcard she is at Liverpool.

The *Peveril* was the first cargo ship specially built for the Steam Packet, and is seen here leaving Douglas. A wheelhouse was only added after an incident in 1934 when the swing bridge in Coburg Dock, Liverpool, removed her mainmast. Captain Philip Bridson of Castletown remembered her worst passage when, laden with cattle and mail and running into a south-westerly gale, they had to run for the Welsh coast. Because of the delay and the state of the tide they berthed in Brunswick Dock to unload the cattle when they eventually reached Liverpool, rather than calling at the landing stage. The next morning the captain read in the morning paper that the *Peveril* had been reported 'missing feared lost' due to his failure to deliver the mails to the usual place. The vessel had her name changed to *Peveril II* in October 1963 for the last few months of her long life, to release her original name for the company's new cargo vessel.

Photographed leaving for Liverpool on her first passenger service, the *Lady of Mann* was the company's centenary steamer and at 3,104 tons, with accommodation for 2,873 passengers, was the largest ship they had owned. She was launched at Barrow by the Duchess of Athol, the 'Lady of Mann' after whom she was named. The accommodation was particularly luxurious having, paradoxically, been built during the slump following the 1929 Wall Street crash when only the most skilled staff had been kept on at the Vickers Armstrong yards. Her tea-room was framed out in sycamore with apple birch panels, the ladies' saloon in mahogany with maple, the first class lounges in veneered mahogany, the first class dining saloon in African walnut and the three saloons on the lower deck in oak and mahogany.

The *Lady of Mann* was painted white for the 1933 season and is seen here at Fleetwood, on her usual pre-war route. On her arrival at Douglas from the builders, the crew of the *Viking*, the previous ship to have served the route, were transferred to her. She carried over 2,000,000 troops during the war years and saw service at the D-Day landings. The *Lady of Mann* was withdrawn from service in August 1971 after a final passage from Ardrossan to Douglas.

Built in 1921 as the *Abingdon* for Cheviot Coasters Ltd. of Newcastle-upon-Tyne, the *Conister* was a single hatch coaster and the last coal-fired vessel in the fleet. She was added to the fleet after becoming stranded at Ramsey on 1 October 1931 and being disposed of by her previous owners, who feared that she would break her back. She was frequently to be seen in Ramsey unloading goods from Liverpool before sailing on to Douglas, where this Stafford Johns photograph was taken. The *Conister* was severely damaged by a bomb during an air attack on 27 October 1940, but survived to serve until 1965.

Built at Cammell Lairds in Birkenhead, the *Mona's Queen* was launched with a white hull in response to the success of the colour scheme on the *Ben-my-Chree* and *Lady of Mann*. Her passenger accommodation included twenty cabins and was advanced for the time. The *Mona's Queen* was tragically lost at Dunkirk on 29 May 1940 when she struck a mine as she entered the harbour on her second trip. Earlier she had been the last merchant ship to leave Calais, having carried in a cargo of high explosives under aerial bombardment. Twenty-four crew, seventeen from the Island, died as she sank.

This Sankeys postcard shows the launch of the *Fenella* at Barrow-in Furness on 16 December 1936. She was built and launched at the same time as her sister ship the *Tynwald IV*, both vessels setting the standard for the classic steamers of the 1940s and 50s. The only obvious difference between the two was that the *Fenella*'s bulwarks were painted black up to the windows of the shelter deck. Her maiden voyage was from Liverpool to Douglas on 1 May 1937.

This port view shows the *Fenella* as new in 1937 with New Brighton pier in the background. Designed primarily for winter service, the *Fenella* was initially used to popularise cheap day excursions on trips to Belfast and Dublin. She was sadly to prove the most short-lived of all Steam Packet vessels, sunk on 30 May 1940 when a bomb fell between the ship and the Dunkirk quay wall. The *Fenella* was broken up where she lay, despite rumours that she had been repaired and placed in service by the Germans.

The *Fenella* had extensive promenade and shelter decks, and this view of the main deck shows the stairs leading up to the shelter deck and down to the lower deck. The main deck contained some third class accommodation – note the gate by the wireless room that would have been used to separate the different classes of passenger.

The *Fenella*'s large public rooms were the last word in passenger ship design and were furnished to a standard that would certainly be the envy of present day passengers. The first class ladies lounge, pictured here, was particularly luxurious, as were the three first class sleeping saloons on the lower deck, each with berths for between 48 and 54 persons.

The second of the new vessels launched in 1936, the *Tynwald*, with her white bulwarks, had a more pleasing appearance than her sister ship. The names *Fenella* and *Tynwald* were chosen to echo the names of the two vessels which had maintained the Island service during the First World War. In 1939 the Manx government reluctantly agreed to allow Sunday excursions from Heysham and the *Tynwald* had the distinction of being the first vessel to land Sunday trippers on the Island. Unfortunately, after a distinguished war service, she was sunk by two torpedoes from the Italian submarine *Argo* on 11 November 1942 with the loss of ten men.